AMERICA'S OFFICIAL JOB SEARCH MANUAL

DEIRK L. KEITT SR.

authorHOUSE®

AuthorHouse™
1663 Liberty Drive
Bloomington, IN 47403
www.authorhouse.com
Phone: 1 (800) 839-8640

© 2019 Deirk L. Keitt Sr. All rights reserved.

No part of this book may be reproduced, stored in a retrieval system, or transmitted by any means without the written permission of the author.

Published by AuthorHouse 08/22/2019

ISBN: 978-1-7283-1910-0 (sc)
ISBN: 978-1-7283-1912-4 (e)

Library of Congress Control Number: 2019909697

Print information available on the last page.

Any people depicted in stock imagery provided by Getty Images are models, and such images are being used for illustrative purposes only.
Certain stock imagery © Getty Images.

This book is printed on acid-free paper.

Because of the dynamic nature of the Internet, any web addresses or links contained in this book may have changed since publication and may no longer be valid. The views expressed in this work are solely those of the author and do not necessarily reflect the views of the publisher, and the publisher hereby disclaims any responsibility for them.

CONTENTS

Acknowledgments ix
Content Overview xi

Chapter 1   The Job Search and Your Emotions 1
Chapter 2   Get Organized 5
Chapter 3   Accessing the Hidden Job Market 8
Chapter 4   Be Adaptable 12
Chapter 5   Produce Effective Tools: Résumé/CV, Cover Letter,
             and Thank-You Letter 15
Chapter 6   Creative Job Searching 31
Chapter 7   Marketing Yourself Effectively 39
Chapter 8   Effective Interview Techniques 44
Chapter 9   How to Follow Up on the Interview 70
Chapter 10   Social Media and the Job Search 73

About the Author 81
About This Manual 83

This book is about acquiring the skills needed to

> find and change jobs;
> market yourself effectively;
> perform well in interviews; and
> follow up on interviews.

Sayings of Wisdom

An investment in knowledge pays the best interest.

—Benjamin Franklin

Knowledge is the only instrument of production that is not subject to diminishing returns.

—J. M. Clarke

A job search seems simple, but the process is complicated to someone untrained and uninformed. Many people fail to realize that a job search is a sport. Like any other sport, you have to develop skills and train. Everyone who plans to succeed in their sport has a coach who lives, eats, sleeps, and dreams their sport.

Well, I live, eat, sleep, dream, and breathe job searches. They are my life, and I love job searches. Even though a job search can be a fun and rewarding learning experience for some, it can be an emotional strain for people who are not trained in it. My system simplifies the process and makes it manageable for anyone, from teens to senior citizens and from those with limited education to those with degrees.

I am Deirk L. Keitt Sr., and I have helped more than ten thousand people over the past eighteen years obtain gainful employment. I have trained, taught, counseled, and coached individuals right into employment.

My assistance was received with appreciation by people of various educational backgrounds. I have assisted people with limited education through individuals with degrees.

This book is a simple "you can do it yourself," handheld manual that you can carry with you while you are job searching.

ACKNOWLEDGMENTS

I'd like to thank my Creator, my heavenly Father.

I dedicate this book to the greatest gifts God has blessed me with: my beautiful, patient, and supporting wife, Esther; our eleven children; and our grandchildren, both born and unborn.

I'd like to also acknowledge Ms. Be-Be Ali, whom I met in physical therapy. She encouraged me to put my passion, helping people in job searching, to print.

Thanks to Ms. Tish Edwards, a former coworker who, by the grace of the Almighty, inspired me to focus attention on an unseen but important population in our community.

I have included some findings and techniques of other job search experts who have been in the business a lot longer than I. I have a great deal of respect for their work and research.

Thank you all.

May you continue to be blessed.

CONTENT OVERVIEW

This job search manual will help you develop your own job search skills to attain any position from entry level to management level. During the past eighteen years, I've consulted for and with several government contract vendors, resulting in thousands of people leaving government programs and acquiring full-time gainful employment, which is the first step to self-sufficiency.

In chapter 1 we discuss one major barrier in particular—your emotions and how to control negative emotions. One way to do that would be to follow the blueprint in chapters 2 through 9 and practice what you learn.

Chapter 2 will help you organize your job search, which is very important. You'll learn to cover more territory and reach more people in a shorter period of time than those who are not organized. It will also help you keep your frustration level down.

Different networking techniques that can be used to reach as many people as possible will be expounded upon in chapter 3. When you combine chapter 2 with chapter 3, you will be very effective in recruiting a vast number of people to assist you in locating job opportunities, far more than if you were working at it alone.

Chapter 4 is short and direct to the point. It will discuss a few pieces of information you will need before an interview and why the information is important.

Chapter 5 covers the tools you need to develop and use in your job search: your résumé/CV, cover letter, and thank-you letter.

Hidden interviews or not-so-obvious interviews sometimes lead to the final decisions; this will be discussed in chapter 6. You will learn why it is crucial to be aware when you're in an informal versus a formal sit-down, question-and-answer interview setting. It also covers the need to be creative in your job search.

Chapter 7 covers how to get a formal job interview set up and the information you need to get when setting up the interview. Chapter 8 details how to use this information you've gotten to open an interview properly in order to take and keep control of the interview. If done right, your confidence will increase as the interview progresses, helping you relax a little more.

To help you further with your interview, we've included some of the top questions asked by recruiters. Some questions we included were why they're asking a particular question and how you can reduce the risk of a failed interview while answering. All this is summed up in chapter 8, which goes on to discuss how to execute a flawless close to the interview.

Chapter 9 deals with what you should do after the interview in order to stand out in the minds of the interviewers. These steps are very important to branding yourself and getting offered a job.

Social media is a very effective tool used in job searches. Chapter 10 discusses some of the social media companies and how they are used in job searches.

CHAPTER 1
THE JOB SEARCH AND YOUR EMOTIONS

A job search will be one of the most emotional roller-coaster experiences you'll ever have. It's in the top five of the most emotional experiences one has to face at some point in life. A job search can be very difficult for you and the important people in your life.

When you stress, whether you know it or not, your family and loved ones feel the effects. Being unemployed can be painful and can leave you with some unpleasant memories. The effects have been devastating to some and left many individuals as well as families scarred. I am not telling you this to scare you. I am quite sure you have enough anxieties to deal with. I'm telling you this to make you aware that you must have a game plan, goals, and values for your job search to be most effective.

You will need a coach with a formula that works. A coach who will assist you in getting back to work as quickly and as painlessly as possible. Again, folks, that's me, Deirk L. Keitt Sr., your personal job search coach.

You want to know the following:

1) Who obtains the best jobs?
2) Who do employers hire?
3) Is it the most qualified? "*No*," say most employment agents and job developers. Employers hire people they like.
4) What can you do to be more liked?
5) How can you be more effective in your job search?

The answers to these questions are exactly what I'm going to show you in this book. Job searches can be one of life's pleasurable learning experiences. First, let us deal with and get rid of the negative realities that cause us to suffer during job searches.

I mentioned anxieties earlier. The first thing I want to do is help you relax your anxiety level. *Anxiety* means to be overly worried about something. Long-term stressful situations may cause anxiety. Learn to relax a little. There is a lot of information on relaxing your anxiety level. Start with your primary care physician.

One major concern is fear of not getting another job. Yes, rejection can add to anxiety. Many people today are reluctant to job search because of the fear of being rejected. These people feel they'll be rejected for many reasons.

Some feel that if they are rejected, they will not be able to maintain the same lifestyle or improve it. Then their own mind starts to play tricks on them, telling themselves that their self-worth has diminished. This can take them into a depressed state of mind. If such a state lasts over a period of time, seek professional help. Job seeking while in a depressed state may not come across well with employers.

Surviving Unemployment

Handling the loss of employment has been likened to walking through a minefield. The book *Parting Company* identifies the most frequent emotions experienced as anger, shame, fear, sadness, and self-pity. Coping with these is difficult. The authors observe: "You've been handed a difficult assignment—determining your future. You haven't asked for this assignment, you probably don't know how to proceed, and all of a sudden you may feel very much alone."

Explaining their sudden dismissal to their family is one of the most difficult problems the unemployed face.

There are some practical ways to deal with the impact of downsizing.

The first step is to downsize your way of life immediately by planning for and living a lifestyle that is simpler than what you have been accustomed to in the past.

Here are some suggestions that may help you to handle the situation, even if they do not solve it altogether.

First, recognize that unexpected job loss is a reality in these times. Regardless of your age and experience, plan ahead for that possibility in the way you live your life.

Second, be careful about taking on any large debt for items that are not essential for sustenance and shelter. Live within your means, and do not assume that you can cover debts with anticipated income from promotions or regular wage increases. The message of today's economy is that there may be no long-term future to rely on.

Third, look for ways to simplify your life and reduce existing financial commitments. This includes shedding debts for items that are not essential to a reasonably simple, wholesome lifestyle.

Fourth, review your lifetime goals and update them. Then you can weigh all decisions against your goals and assess their impact.

Fifth and finally, do not look longingly at the lifestyle of others in your community who are living less frugally, lest you begin to desire the things they have and be lured into their way of life.

Keep Life Simple and Uncluttered Manage Your Time and Set Priorities

Determine which things are the most important, and assign sufficient time to these. In setting priorities, take into account your need for a little solitude—time for constructive meditation and for recharging your own batteries. Meaningful alone time is time well spent.

Get ready to put in work finding employment. Job searching is a job itself.

Staying busy doing something you know will pay off with positive results will always reduce anxiety levels. Getting employed is definitely a positive result.

You can reduce your anxieties over job searching. Look at each successful stage of the job search as an accomplishment that puts you one step closer to reaching your employment goals. For example, you get a job lead. That is an accomplishment. Next, an interview is set for you, again another successful step. Also keep in mind that getting prepared and acquiring the proper tools are all steps of success getting you closer to your job.

Employer Fears

My research has discovered that employers who are looking to hire have fears of their own. They have even more reasons to fear than you, the job seeker, have. The reason they have more fear is they have more at risk than we do. For example, if they hire the wrong person, they can lose a lot, such as

- good employees;
- insurance;
- contracts;
- investments;
- revenue;
- products/merchandise;
- business;
- health; and
- life.

Your goal is to eliminate their fears of hiring you.

Well, how do I do that? you may be wondering. Stop stressing; I am going to teach you how to do just that.

CHAPTER 2
GET ORGANIZED

There are a great number of things you need to organize to conduct a successful job search. These include your schedule, your tools, your clothing, your method of travel, and your meals and rest.

Organize Your Schedule

One thing that will help you reduce stress is establishing your own workday schedule. Never forget that a job search is a job; it's work. Like any other job, being organized can help eliminate waste. You don't want to waste any time or resources. Organizing yourself will also help you to chart any progress in reaching your goal. So write your schedule down. Check it daily. Plan your job search for each day the day or night before.

Organize Your Tools

Among the tools you need to organize are

- your résumé;
- your cover letter;
- your thank-you letter;
- black pens and # 2 pencils;
- your certificates, degrees, licenses, and transcripts;
- a master application and business cards;

- briefcase or portfolio; and
- telephone book (study your phone book; get to know it).

Send out résumés and set up interviews in an organized fashion. Categorize them by

- mode of sending (email, faxing, postal mail);
- deadline response time;
- type of job; and
- address and zip code area.

Organize Your Clothing

Prepare your clothes the night before or for the entire week. Being dressed for success and being organized will heighten your confidence, make you a little more relaxed, and help eliminate some of the negative emotions. This is true even if you decide to use a day just to make phone calls. When you're dressed up, you'll feel and even sit differently. You won't lie down to make your calls, and this will reflect in your phone voice; it is very important how you sound to the person on the other end of the phone.

Organize Your Method of Travel

- When doing direct business contacts, schedule if possible by address in a systematic way to cover as many stops as you can make with as little downtime as possible.
- Contact transportation networks. Download maps. If you're using public transportation, find out when public transportation is accessible and less crowded. (Waiting long periods for a bus or train can increase anxiety.)
- If you're driving, make sure you have the necessary fuel for your travel day and drive when there are fewer cars on the streets and highways. (The fear of running out of fuel while stuck in traffic sends most people's anxiety level soaring.)

Schedule Your Meals and Rest

Scheduling meals and rest will reduce fatigue and stress. Be sure to stick to your schedule.

Good eating habits, such as when, what, and how to eat to reduce stress levels, can be found on health sites on the internet. Also get information on this from your primary care physician. You can also talk to a certified nutritionist.

CHAPTER 3

ACCESSING THE HIDDEN JOB MARKET

When fishing, if you use the largest net, you're more likely to catch the most fish.

If you increase the size of your network, you improve your chances of finding work. *Network, network, network.*

Everyone you talk to is a potential job lead. If you respond only to news ads and internet ads, you are narrowing your chances. The majority of jobs may be slipping right by your net if it is too small. Many jobs are never advertised. You have to access the hidden job market. *How?*

Responding to internet and classified ads is good, but incorporate other avenues of job searching. Set aside time to contact businesses you think may have jobs you can do.

Network with everyday working people who, in their daily work, contact many other people and businesses. Just one example of many: messengers go in and out of businesses every day and all day. They spend time talking with receptionists, who know everyone and sometimes everything going on in the company they work for and the companies they do business with. Don't forget about gas station attendants. You should especially consider this if you're a person who fills up your gas tank at the same gas station around the same time every week. If you and the gas attendant have gotten to know each other, then more than likely, there are other customers the attendant has gotten to know. In a short period of time, the attendant could come across some information valuable to a job seeker, information such as what new businesses are opening up or moving into your designated job area.

Another example is truckers and delivery persons. They travel from business to business with information that could help you land a job. During the period that I owned my own janitorial maintenance company, I was in the office of a supermarket when one trucker in conversation told the bookkeeper that a supermarket on his route was letting their bookkeeper go the following week. At another time, in the same supermarket, a trucker, while explaining why he was making his delivery late, told the manager he had to wait until another supermarket manager found people to unload his truck because he had fired some of his workers that morning and was therefore short-staffed.

That's when I first realized that people who go from business to business carry a great deal of valuable information for job seekers.

Also, I realized that store managers and their staff who work where myself and others like me have been spending our hard-earned money collect a lot of valuable information.

They have a large resource pool. Just look at those thousands of items in a supermarket. There are hundreds of companies that make and deliver products to the local supermarkets. The managers and owners have a working relationship and contact with these businesses.

Just one product has so many jobs within various departments attached to it. For example, all these departments contain one or more positions depending on the size of the company and its needs:

- Administration
- Human Resources
- Sales and Marketing
- Information Technology
- Labor, Distribution, and Delivery
- Security

- Cleaning and Maintenance
- Legal

So if you're looking for a job in food service, ask yourself, Would a supermarket owner or manager have the connections? Is it likely that his manufacturers and distributors are selling food and food products to kitchens in nursing homes, hospitals, schools, catering companies, and airlines, just to name a few? I'm sure they are.

This local community of stores, manufacturers, and distributing companies want you and me to keep working so we can keep buying their products. Therefore, they'd be willing to use their precious networking system to at least keep their eyes and ears open for the purpose of helping you get back to work. So put them to work. Add them to your network list.

Start by recruiting the businesses in your community where you live and spend your money. These supermarkets along with many other businesses are seen as distribution centers for the manufacturers and wholesalers. Therefore, the businesses where you spend your money are your connection to hundreds, even thousands, of people in the work world.

If you ask them, they'll contact their distributors and network for you. The more people you have woven into your network system, the larger your net becomes, and the better opportunity you have to catch more fish. With more fish in your net, you have more choices. That is, choices of jobs.

Referrals, an Important Part of Networking

Don't forget referrals. Ask anyone who says he or she has no work available, "Where else can I look or to whom can I ask who would have these types of positions?" If they give you someone or someplace to try, ask them if you can use their name. If they suggest a company in the same or a related industry, that could be a plus for you. Remember—if they've been in this industry or a related one for some time, they may have established a good reputation. If that is the case, their name and reputation may be the thing to get you in the door for an interview or, better, the job.

The July 8, 2000, issue of *Awake* magazine had an article entitled "How to Find a Job and Keep It." In this article you'll find examples of people who used this method.

The first one was a man named Tony, who took the initiative to contact a company even though they were not advertising job openings. He explained one company said they had no jobs at present, but he should try again in three months. He did, and he gained employment.

Primrose, a single mom from South Africa, also widened her net. "While I was attending a first aid course," she said, "I noticed a building under construction across the road and discovered it was going to be a nursing home for the elderly. I tried several times to set an appointment with the superintendent of the facility. He finally told me there currently were no jobs. I kept returning to see if I could work there even as a volunteer. Eventually I was hired on a temp basis. I applied myself to whatever assignment I was given. As a result, I gained additional qualifications and obtained a permanent position at the facility."

Please do not forget your family, friends, and people in your community. These people may not have jobs where they work, but they may know where a position is available or may know someone who knows someone who knows someone who knows someone who knows someone who knows someone who has a position. Be reminded of the rule of six degrees of separation; you're that close to getting the job you want.

CHAPTER 4
BE ADAPTABLE

While I was teaching and coaching in how to job search, a job developer came into my classroom one afternoon and announced he had a position for a foot messenger and the interview was set for the following day. Out of approximately forty job seekers, only one young man embraced the opportunity. He went with the job developer to his office to get all the details. He came back about fifteen minutes later, excited and ready to start getting ready for that interview on the following day. So I excused him for the rest of the day.

He packed his belongings, came over to my desk, and said something that I've included in my lessons from that day forward. He said, "I'm going to get paid while job searching." I didn't understand. So I asked him, "What do you mean?" He told me he was in the market for a computer programmer job, but he was taking this position because it allowed him access to people and offices he could not just walk into. As a messenger he'd be in and out of offices all over New York City. He said he'd dress comfortable casual, keep a few résumés with him, and once he'd visited an office a few times and established a little rapport, he would present his résumé and tell them what type of position he was looking for. He gave himself two months but reached his goal in less time. He was successful in such a short period of time because he was willing to adapt.

The ability to adapt increases your chances of getting employed as quickly as possible. You may not find the job you want with everything you want in a job. You need to learn to adapt and be content until you can get the job you actually want.

Being adaptable may mean the difference between feeding yourself or going hungry. It will mean getting rid of any prejudices you have toward different types of jobs. Feeding yourself could mean doing a combination of jobs also. Don't be adamant about doing the same type of work that you have been doing.

In this economy it is an employer's market, so you may have to learn how to use jobs as stepping-stones to get to the job you want. For example, one of my former students took a job in a fast-food restaurant long enough to pay for his commercial driving course. Once he obtained his CDL license, he left fast food and went into truck driving. Another student took the home health aide course and then worked with an HHA company long enough to get in the union and had the union pay for her nursing degree.

I once took a job as a dietary aide in a nursing home. I had just graduated from a cooking school. I applied for a position as a cook with this nursing home. They only had dietary aide positions available, with the prospect of a long-term temporary cook's position opening in six months.

I thought about it quickly. The nursing home was a union shop. I could get plenty of overtime. I could move into a cook's position as soon as one became available, and I was engaged to be married in a year. After I was taken on a tour of the kitchen and introduced to potential coworkers, I realized two of the cooks and the head chef were definitely near retirement age.

I rolled the dice on this one and was right. In six months I was working the cook station while one cook was out on sick leave. When his six-month leave was almost up, he had it extended another six months. During that period of time, another cook retired, and I became a permanent cook. What a beautiful wedding gift! That was what I wanted, a cook's job. Had

I turned down the dietary aide position because it wasn't what I wanted, I would not have been there when the position I wanted became available.

These are just a few examples out of many where individuals used one job to get to the job they really wanted. Follow up on job opportunities that come along, whether it is something you've done before or not and even if it's something you don't want to do. At least try to find out what other job opportunities, now and in the near future, are available.

CHAPTER 5

PRODUCE EFFECTIVE TOOLS: RÉSUMÉ/CV, COVER LETTER, AND THANK-YOU LETTER

Résumé

For any position, including an executive position, compiling and distributing a professional résumé is a must. In some places similar documents are called a CV or curriculum vitae. No matter what the position is, a positive, well-prepared résumé is a must. It is truly an asset. It will tell potential employers who you are, what you've accomplished, where you've been, and where you are going. In other words, it pretty much tells what circles you've traveled in and why they need you. However, too many times people have shown me what they consider a résumé, but I call them resumes, something that will cause you to resume your position back on unemployment.

Here is an example of what I mean. The first entry is frequently where the employment history begins and in most cases where the problem with the résumé begins. A resume may say something like this:

ABC Cleaning /Maintenance Inc. 01/01/01–02/02/02

Janitor

Empty garbage. Clean bathrooms. Clean offices. Sweep floors. Mop floors. Vacuum.

Well by now I know you've got the point. These are just a few of the minor problems I find with what some call a résumé.

Some of you may have already zeroed in on the problem. But I have found that most people who think they know how to create a winning résumé see no problem with this. This applies also to people who've been working for years and people who have spent their time getting degrees, as well as the people who are limited in work experience and those short on education.

For those who are wondering, what's the problem? Here it is. Based on this person's resume, I don't have a clue how much of anything this person did.

I do not know if this person emptied one little garbage basket per shift or fifty thirty-to-seventy-five-gallon trash receptacles per shift.

I do not know if this person cleaned one bathroom per week or cleaned and sanitized ten stall-bathrooms with five urinals, eight bathrooms per floor in a ten-story building every day or twice a day.

A valuable résumé will give a good picture of what you've done and how much work you've done. Provide details of previous work history. Include examples of goals you've reached and the benefits you brought to former employers.

I have included two different types of résumés as examples on the next two pages of this manual.

John A. Doe

999 Main Street, Ann Arbor, MI 99999
(123) 555-1234
johndoe@email.com

CAREER OBJECTIVE

Experienced and versatile professional with strong urban planning as well as people, management, and research skills seeks a position in urban planning and environmental impact analysis with a major city or Fortune 500 company.

CORE QUALIFICATIONS

- Background managing direct transportation planning and programs
- Adept at managing programs and people
- Able to anticipate and project organizational change
- Background as administrator of office operations

EXPERIENCE AND SKILLS

Skilled in Government Guidelines • Quality Control • Urban Planning • Environmental Impact Mitigation and Research • Urban Planning • Geology/Hydrology • Site Evaluations • Computer Software Tools • Scientific and Business Grant Writing

Administrative: Lead coordinator for the daily processing of thousands of checks for payment and the mailing of confidential reports, meeting strict deadlines, and avoiding late fees.

Problem Solving: Designed a waste-management program involving Recycle Ann Arbor and a major book company, intended for the efficient handling of tons of paper, cardboard, plastic, metal, and glass, achieving net savings of $20,000 per building annually and reducing company disposal obligations.

Management: Oversaw operations of an expanding research lab, providing expertise, commitment, and quality control during a time of significant transition.

EMPLOYMENT HISTORY

Senior Process Engineer, September 2016-Present, Zezee Corp., Ann Arbor, Mich.
Process Engineer: Technical Support, September 2012-September 2016, Zezee Corp., Ann Arbor, Mich.
Technical Professional**,** September 2010-September 2012, City of the Stars, Mich.

EDUCATION

Master of Business Administration (2015); GPA 3.9
Southern Nazarene University, Bethany, Okla. (Online Program)

Bachelor of Science (Emphasis: Ecosystem/Environmental Business) May 2012
Eastern Michigan University, Ypsilanti, Michigan

James Applicant
17017 Home Blvd. • Edmond, OR 00222 • (555) 555-1212 • james.applicant@email.com

---

OVERVIEW

Energetic and motivating leader with a proven ability to effectively manage both staff and long and short-term projects. A self-starter and strong independent worker who excels at analyzing products and procedures in order to generate new ideas that improve efficiency and production quality.

PROFESSIONAL EXPERIENCE

COMFORT, INC., *Edmond, OR*
MANAGER (2014-Present)

Manage daily operations of a $1 million foam insulation company.

- Train and supervise work crews in more efficient product installation techniques resulting in reduced material waste by 20 percent and labor hours by 43 percent.
- Instrumental in developing sales team's knowledge in the areas of building science and energy conservation in order to provide customers with the information to successfully plan for, and utilize, spray foam insulation.

MILITARY BASE. Edmond, OR
DATA NETWORK MANAGER (2012-2014)

Managed command and control data network used to generate video representation of geographic area surrounding the ship. The team consisted of 38 individuals from four departments.

- Production Control Officer - Coordinated the efforts of 135 personnel utilizing 37,000 man hours. Completed 520 jobs totaling over $4 million during a 13-month refurbishment period.
- Assistant Command Duty Officer - Directed daily routine utilizing a duty section of 600 personnel from 12 different departments.

MILITARY BASE. *Edmond, OR*
INSTRUCTOR PILOT (2008–2012)

Administered, coordinated, and supervised flight and academic training for the United States flight training program that encompassed over 200 instructors and 600 students in five units.

- Coordinated and supervised four Flight Commanders to ensure that pilot completion rates met quarterly and annual goals.
- Managed and scheduled 11 instructor pilots and 38 flight students to complete primary and intermediate level flight training.

EDUCATION

AUBURN UNIVERSITY, MBA in Finance, 2018
UNIVERSITY OF COSTA RICA, Bachelor of Arts in Business Economics, 2004
Aviator - Advanced Flight Training, United States Flight Patrol

Did you

- increase profits;
- reduce downtime;
- shrink overhead cost; or
- eliminate waste?

If you did, indicate that you did, for whom you did it, and how much you did. Put in the numbers.

Highlight aspects of previous jobs that qualify you for the position you are applying for. Please include information that will describe your qualities, interests, and extracurricular activities.

Because needs differ from company to company, you may have to adjust your résumé with each application. A good résumé helps you prepare and organize your goals and thoughts.

Cover Letter

Sayings of Wisdom

Find the good—and praise it.

—Alex Haley

I've seen what people thought were cover letters. Some I told, "You can use that to cover up things around the house, but don't give that thing you call a cover letter to anyone." To put together a winning cover letter, you must first know the purpose of the letter. The purpose of a cover letter is to introduce you when you cannot be there in person, set you aside as different from your competitors, and tell why you are the person they should hire. Now you might be wondering, "Exactly when should I send my cover letter?" You send the cover letter only when you're faxing, mailing, or emailing your résumé to a potential employer.

There is, of course, an exception to the rule. You can leave a cover letter with a résumé at a place of business if someone tells you to leave your résumé with them and they'll pass it on to someone in particular whom you spoke to them about. Make sure the name of the person for whom the résumé is intended is correctly spelled on the cover letter.

Always be sure to sign your letter. I've seen many beautiful cover letters in my days, unsigned. You must sign your cover letters. The cover letter should always capture the employer's interest in the beginning, and you should always state your qualifications in the first line along with the position you are seeking.

Next, you'll let them know what qualities and skills you've used, developed, or enhanced, and on what jobs. Tell them the benefits you provided to those former companies you worked for.

Also tell them things you've learned, know, and like about their company, such as their goals, mission, agenda, or community relations. Then you'll let them know why you're a perfect match. It's just like when you want to date someone, you know, when you're just in that talking about it stage. Don't you always tell that person what you've learned about them and what you like about them and why the two of you would be perfect together? It's basically the same when you're trying to make a marriage alliance with a company you want to work with.

Finally, when you are at the end of your cover letter, what do you do? Ask them to contact you via telephone or email. Keep it simple.

I have included below a sample of an acceptable cover letter and a sample of a cover letter that in most cases would not get read after the first line. They will give you a good idea on how to set up a cover letter that will get read. It is a waste of the employer's time, your time, and ink and paper telling them you're writing them about a position they're advertising. First, they know why you're writing since you sent the résumé with the cover letter. Second, there is no need to mention anything about their advertisement; since they spent the time and money to place the ad, they are already quite aware of their own advertisement.

Remember that for every job you apply for, hundreds to thousands of people are going for that same job. So if an employer has a thousand cover letters in front of him to read, he or she will not waste time reading a cover letter that is telling them things they already know. If they don't finish reading your cover letter, they will not pick up your résumé. If they don't pick up your résumé, they will not contact you. Remember that your phone number and email address are on that résumé; you want them to pick up that résumé, read it, and call you.

But they'll look at the résumé only if the cover letter gets their interest.

Sample Cover Letters

Your Contact Information
Name
Address
City, State Zip Code
Phone Number
Cell Phone Number
Email

Ms. Ophelia Lee
Human Resources Director
Acme Windows
123 Business Rd.
Business City, NY 54321

Date

Dear Ms. Lee,

In today's customer service oriented society, timely, friendly, proactive service is sought to enhance future business growth. Customer loyalty is always impacted when you employ the right service professional to represent you when assisting your valued customers.

My long-term experience in the service industry has taught me how to meet and exceed each customer's expectations with service that sells. I have assisted all types of customers in all types of settings. I realize that acquiring and maintaining loyal repeat business as well as spreading the word of your business through these loyal patrons is of the utmost importance in every company.

Positioning a company for better exposure and greater marketability is a task that I have performed with success many times. I am an excellent trainer who achieves ongoing success with her teams by building morale, maintaining teams' self-confidence, and training them to build the sale by improving their people skills.

It would be a pleasure to interview with you and I look forward to hearing from you soon.
Very sincerely,

Your Signature (on a hard-copy letter)

Your Typed Name

Finance Internship Cover Letter Example

Your Contact Information
Name
Address
City, State Zip Code
Phone Number
Cell Phone Number
Email

Employer Contact Information
Name
Title
ABC Financial Group
Address
City, State Zip Code

Date

Dear Mr./Ms. Last Name:

Education, training, and a keen eye for details are needed to succeed in the financial industry. If that is the type of person you're looking to invest in, look no farther; I am the person you want.

My experiences have provided me with a detailed knowledge of financial institutions and have enhanced my interest in pursuing a financial career.

Through ABC Financial Group's website, I learned about your bank's present career opportunities.

I am extremely interested in securing a position in the ABC Financial Group's Global Equity Summer Internship Program. I am currently in my second year at the Smith Business School of the State University and am concentrating in finance, accounting, and real estate. Over the summer I completed an internship with First National Bank and am currently interning with the University's Student Federal Credit Union.

I feel that an internship with ABC Financial Group would be a logical next step in my development as an investment banker.

My main interest in joining ABC Financial Group stems from its impressive reputation. The prestige of the firm is best captured through its recent decoration as "America's Most Trusted Corporation" for the second consecutive year. I feel the firm's diverse clientele, large market capitalization, and well-established summer internship program would provide me with an invaluable experience to complement my studies at Business School.

I believe that I would succeed in the firm's exciting and motivated environment and that my strong work ethic, ability, and passion would make me a valuable asset to your firm.

I would prefer to work in global equity; however, I am willing to consider any position that you offer me. Thank you for your consideration, and I look forward to speaking with you in the near future.

Sincerely,

Your Signature (on a hard-copy letter)

Your Typed Name

Transferable Sales Skills Cover Letter Example

Your Contact Information
Name
Address
City, State Zip Code
Phone Number
Cell Phone Number
Email

Employer Contact Information
Name
Title
Company
Address
City, State Zip Code

Date

Dear Hiring Manager,

Retail merchandising, customer service strategies, and business communications are just a few of the skills needed to succeed in retail management. If this is the type of employee you would like to invest in, look no farther; I'm your gal.

In reviewing your corporate website, I was excited to learn about your management training program. Please consider the attached résumé as a sign of my very deep interest in becoming an intern in this exciting program.

During my undergraduate studies in business administration at ABC College, I have enjoyed the opportunity to explore subjects including retail merchandising, customer service strategies, and business communications—studies that have inspired me to pursue a career in retail management.

To this end, I have worked for our campus bookstore for the past six months as a salesclerk, acquiring a solid knowledge of how to provide excellence in customer service. My duties in this role have also included merchandising, stocking, and inventory control.

I believe that as an intern in your management training program, my enthusiasm for customer service and retail sales will become clear.

Also, I look forward to using my leadership skills (developed as captain of the ABC College Crew Team and Rush Chairman for my sorority) to learn how to motivate and coordinate store teams, with an emphasis upon honesty, diversity, inclusion, and safety. Other skills I have that will transfer well to this role include:

> *Excellent verbal and nonverbal communications talents, with fluency in both English and Spanish.*
> *A demonstrated attention to accuracy in all cash and credit handling transactions, with the ability to quickly master new POS systems.*
> *A dedication to team building and accomplishment, based on creating a climate of mutual respect among all team members, no matter what their position or level of seniority.*

Thank you for your time and consideration in reviewing the attached résumé; I would be grateful for the opportunity to speak with you directly in a personal interview. Please let me know if there is any additional information I can provide in support of my candidacy for this internship.

Sincerely,

Your Signature (on a hard-copy letter)

Your Typed Name

Thank-You Letter

Dear Raquel,

Thank you so much for being a source of encouragement to me. Even though you may not know it, your upbuilding nature and kind words have meant a lot.
—Jennifer

- Have you ever received an unexpected note of gratitude? If so, such an expression no doubt warmed your heart. After all, it is natural to want to feel valued and appreciated.
- Regrettably, personal expressions of gratitude, verbal and written, seem to be increasingly rare. If we are not alert, the pervasive lack of gratitude evident today could smother any tender feelings of appreciation that may rise in us.
- After an interview, whether it's over the phone, through video chat, or in person, you should always send a thank-you letter to your interviewer. Sending one is good manners.
- Sending thank-you letters shows appreciation to the person you're thanking for whatever they've done for you. It's common courtesy and shows respect to tell someone who has taken some time out of their busy schedule to show some interest in you, *thank you*!
- The problem is that most people who do attempt to say thanks in job searching think they're sending thank-you letters only because

they feel or were told they had to say something. Be wise and *say something specific* in your thank-you letter.

To stand out as different, you must do things a little differently from the rest of the pack.

Like the cover letter, the thank-you letter should be addressed to someone in particular. "To whom should I address it?" some might ask. What about the employer who allows you to fill out an application even though they told you they had no positions available? Thank that employer for allowing you to fill out one of the applications and considering you.

Also, you should thank the interviewer and anybody else who puts you another step closer to reaching your employment goals.

Be specific. Tell the interviewer about all the things you liked that occurred in, around, or during your interview that would enhance your job performance.

For example:

- Did they allow you to sit before the interview for a few minutes in the waiting area or receptionist area, where you were able to observe some of the daily operations of their company?
- Maybe they took you on a tour of the facility, giving you a detailed description of what your job would entail.
- They could have taken you around the jobsite and introduced you to potential coworkers, making you feel welcome already.
- You could thank them for testing you or making you aware of the things you need to improve.

These are just some of the things you could and should thank them for in your thank-you letter. As you go through your job search, you will accumulate many more reasons to thank your potential employers.

Thanking them for specifics is very important. It will set you apart from those people who don't pay attention to details. Don't just thank them for the interview alone if you want to stand out as different from the rest of the job seekers who do just that. Your thank-you letter does not have to be lengthy. But it should not be merely a thank-you note. The more you have to thank them for, the more they'll take your thank-you letter seriously.

Keep in mind that your tools for a job search reflect who you are. If employers take your tools (résumé, cover letter, and thank-you letter) seriously, then they will take you seriously. When it's time to say thank you, say, "Thank you! Thank you! Thank you!"

Sample Thank-You Note

Hello, <Interviewer's Name>,

I wanted to thank you for your time <yesterday/Friday/etc.>. I enjoyed our conversation about <specific topic you discussed> and enjoyed learning about the <Job Title> position overall.

It sounds like an exciting opportunity, and an opportunity I could succeed and excel in! I'm looking forward to hearing any updates you can share. Don't hesitate to contact me if you have any questions or concerns in the meantime. Thanks again for the great conversation <yesterday/Friday/etc.>.

Best Regards,

<Your Name>

This is obviously a very short, casual message. In tech recruiting, companies are *not* very formal. They use email (or even Google chat), and they keep it brief.

While the sample thank-you note above could be sent in the mail as a letter, it's best as an email after your interview. And it's best when interviewing at start-ups, technology companies, or other modern companies. Such companies will *not* want to see a formal, five-paragraph thank-you letter that takes up a full page. In fact, it might make them want to hire you less.

For more traditional companies, you should send a formal thank-you letter after an interview.

Sample Thank-You Letter

Your Contact Information
Name
Address
City, State Zip Code
Phone Number
Cell Phone Number
Email

Employer Contact Information
Name
Title
Company
Address
City, State Zip Code

Date

Hello, <Interviewer's Name>,

Thank you for taking the time to speak with me <yesterday/Friday/etc.> about the <Job Title> position at <Company Name>. It was a pleasure talking with you, and I really enjoyed hearing all the details you shared about the opportunity.

The information you shared about <something specific about the job that interests you> sounded particularly interesting.

I am confident that my skills will allow me to come in and succeed in this role, and it's a position I'd be excited to take on.

I'm looking forward to hearing from you about the next steps, and please don't hesitate to contact me in the meantime if you have any questions.
Thank you again, and I hope to hear from you soon.

Best Regards,

<Your Name>

CHAPTER 6
CREATIVE JOB SEARCHING

Earlier I said employers hire people they like. Then I asked the question "What can you do to be liked more?" I didn't mean to be liked personally. An employer doesn't have to like you personally, but it's important they like you for the job. If the employer sees that you are a good fit and will suit the company's goals, agenda, customers, and other employees, they will hire you.

There are many ways to impress employers.

Being creative in your job search is one way to impress employers. To be creative means to employ nontraditional techniques in your job search to stand out as different and stay on the minds of the employers you target.

In this chapter I'm going to relate to you some experiences of former students I had the privilege of coaching in job searching. (Names have been changed to protect confidentiality.) However, I want you to know that not every creative technique used here will work with every employer every time it is used. The following experiences are to stimulate your creativity into action. With your knowledge of the industry, position, and hiring manager/manager of the position you're going after, you can come up with some of your own creative techniques. Please contact us and share them.

The first person whose experience I want to share came to our program with a bachelor's degree and more than ten years of professional work experience in corporate America. However, like many of us, she fell on some hard times. She had to apply for public assistance, and that is how she ended up with us. Because of the sensitivity of her case, I have changed her name.

We'll call her Ms. Johnson. While she was in our job search program, we only had to polish her up so to speak with a few pointers. She was already self-motivated, so half the job was done. Without delay she'd go in the field every day to job search. Ms. Johnson was in search of an executive administrative position. She searched day in and day out without letup. She had various successful interviews. One in particular really piqued her interest, and she said, "I really would like to work and grow with that company."

The only problem was because it was a high-level executive position she was applying for, she had to interview with the vice president, who was always too busy to set an appointment.

When someone in her situation applies for public assistance and is unemployed when their case is opened to receive benefits, they will often receive a work assignment to work for their benefits.

After what seemed like a few short weeks to me but eons to her, her case did become open, and she did get an assignment. The moment she received her assignment, she began to show how frustrated she was. She started crying, ripped up the assignment information sheet, and stormed out of the office repeating, "I will get a real job," over and over again. Here is what she related happened after she left our office. She took the subway system home. While riding, she began to reflect on the last few weeks since she'd started her job search. Then it hit her.

It was something she had heard in my class but previously thought it was not necessary for her to apply. *Be creative!* Yes, I've always emphasized being creative in job searching. Although she ignored this before, it did not take her long to come up with a very creative idea.

Sometimes we can come up with the best ideas when we feel our backs are up against the walls and we have nothing more to lose. This is how she described what she was feeling during this period in her life. And boy, did she prove it.

Even though this was more than ten years ago, I today still feel this was one of the most creative ideas I've heard. This is what she did. She went home and got a shoebox. She put one old but not worn-out shoe in the box with her résumé and a note addressed to the busy VP of the company she really wanted to work for. She got back on the subway and went to the office building of that company.

This woman walked up to the security desk, told the desk attendant whom the package was intended for, and turned and walked out, heading for the subway home.

She related to me that as she entered her home, her telephone was ringing. It was the VP herself wanting to know if she could be in the office the very next morning at nine o'clock sharp. She agreed without hesitation. By the way, the VP had already left a few messages on her voice mail.

She informed me that the very next morning when she entered the receptionist/waiting area in the office and identified herself, another individual began calling to the other workers to come meet the lady who had sent the shoe. Little did she know beforehand that her creative idea would have such a profound effect on so many people at this company. She had a reputation with the workers already, and she wasn't even hired yet. When she finished all the introductions and greetings, she was summoned into the VP's office for a formal interview.

Lo and behold, there was a familiar sight. An open shoebox with a résumé sat on top of a shoe, with a note to the side. After gesturing to her to take a seat, the VP reached into the box, took out the note, and began to read. The note read, "Now that I have one foot in the door, please help me get the other foot in." Long story short, she did get hired. Could you imagine what was going through the mind of that VP?

"This woman is a go-getter. Someone who will do almost anything to get the job done." And that she did. Her job was to get a job. She used a creative technique. *She got hired! So can you! Be creative!*

Again, keep in mind that not every method of creative job search will work with every employer every time it is used.

The next person I'd like to tell you about is a young lady who was searching for a position as a childcare provider in a day care setting. We'll call her Lisa. Lisa came to me one day with the look of disappointment and despair on her face. But she had no look of defeat.

She told me that everyone whom she contacted on her list refused to give her an interview. Her determination to go after jobs she thought she was being rejected from helped me to see the type of qualities and character that are needed to succeed in a job search. First is the ability to distinguish an objection from a rejection. Everyone she spoke to brought up an objection (no experience, no early childhood education). No one told her they just didn't want her, which would have been a rejection. They implied there were things standing between her and an interview for the child care position, namely her lack of education and hands-on experience.

Because she did not have early childhood education nor did she have hands-on training in an institutional setting, I tried without success to steer her in another direction, to go after jobs where she fit their requirements. She refused based on something I'd told her and other students.

I had told them how I used creative techniques and got the job I was then working in. I let them know I won the position over seven qualified candidates with degrees and experience. And all I had was a GED, life skills, and a creative mind.

In order for me to get the very job I was then doing, I decided to set myself aside from the rest of the students and stay on the minds of as many people employed there as possible. The first thing I did was start walking and talking like I worked there already. I would borrow a clipboard, put paper in it, pull out a pen, and walk the halls during breaks.

I would ask students questions about their experience there and what changes they would like to see in the program. Then I would write it down. I became visible to the students within a week.

All the students began to think I was staff. So they would come to me with questions. Even if I knew the answer, I would send them to an office or classroom to a particular staff member and tell them to say, "Deirk sent me." After a couple of weeks of "Deirk sent me," I became popular among staff. Even some of them approached and ask if I was the new hire. Staff then started encouraging me to apply there, and of course, with a few more steps, I got the job. Oh, by the way, I didn't get the first position I applied for.

Back to my student who reminded me of this experience that I had shared with the class. After she reminded me of what I had told the students, I gave up trying to deter her. It's then that I realized why she didn't come to me with a defeated look on her face. She realized I was a coach, something I had not realized before. As with any other coach, I had to encourage, not discourage. While her confidence was up was the best time for me to assist, counsel, fortify, and do all those other things coaches do to create winners.

I knew I had a winner. I had to assist her in showing employers she had education and experience in early childcare. "What early childhood education and experience?" you may be asking yourself. Lisa had a five-year-old daughter. When raising a child properly, you will get a lot of education and experience in early childhood. And she already had five years of experience under her belt. She needed to get in an interview and relate to them all the things she did for her client (her daughter) those five years and how her client benefited. Then she could tell them how it all related to the position she was applying for and the benefit it would be to their customers and their company to have her employed in their facility. I knew if she was going to get in, she had to be creative.

This was a very crucial moment in her job search and my career. If you fall from the lower step of a ladder, it will be less painful than when you have already climbed all the way to the top and then fall. A fall from the top can be severe, even fatal. This young lady was at the top of her job search. The last thing she or I needed was for her to tumble down. She could lose her confidence and her rhythm. She could also lose confidence in me or become totally dependent on me or the system to do her job search. My goal and commitment to coach someone in job searching is a goal and commitment to help the student learn job search skills and techniques to become self-sufficient, an effective, independent job seeker.

When I say self-sufficient, I do not mean you'll never be out of work. What I do mean is you will have all the skills and techniques you need to find employment as quickly and as painlessly as possible on your own.

It's about time I get to the creative part of our journey. A few days after she initially came to me with her concerns, I was inspired with a thought. Of course, this was after much prayer. So I asked her, "Do you have any money?" Her response was, "Yes, of course I do."

I told her to take ten dollars and go to the ninety-nine cent store around the corner. "Buy ten children pop-up books and bring them back here to the classroom." I hope you all know what pop-up books are. Just in case you don't, it's all right; I'll tell you. Pop-up books are the books children love because everything stands up on the pages, like animals, vehicles, buildings, and so on. Scenes seem to come alive.

She did exactly what I told her to do. Then I told her to take her résumés and staple one résumé to the middle pop-up page in each book. After she did that, I gave her little stickers. I instructed her to write these words on each sticker: "To the personnel office or person in charge of hiring." Next I coached her on what she should do and say. I told her to take her list of people who refused her initially and go to each one until she had gotten rid of all ten books.

It wasn't going to be easy because I instructed her not to converse with anyone. She was to just talk her way into personnel offices, say a brief greeting to everyone, such as "good morning" or "good afternoon," slap a pop-up book down on a desk, and then turn and leave.

I'm excited to tell you the results. Before I do, let me tell what I figured would happen. Trusting the nature of people, I figured someone would ask, "Who was that, and what is it that she left on the desk?" I assumed someone would go pick it up and open it, and then her résumé would pop out in their face. Someone would go around the workplace showing off her résumé and saying something like, "Look at what some crazy person did."

I didn't care what they called her as long as she was getting the attention needed. I figured eventually they would bring it to the attention of someone with authority and wisdom who would say to themselves, "If she could get and hold the attention of so many people who never met her, there is a strong possibility she could get and hold children's attention." Three days later her phone was ringing for interviews.

To make a long story shorter, out of all the companies that wanted to hire her, she chose (yes, that is correct: she now had choices) the company that made her an offer she said she could not refuse. They offered her a fair entry-level salary and an opportunity to go to school for her early childhood degree at their expense. And then once she'd finished getting her degree, she could stay on board with their team.

Now the results. Excitedly she came into my classroom with great news a few days after dropping off those books. Everyone she left a book with was calling. We don't know if all of them wanted to or would have hired her. But she got their attention, she accepted an offer, and she got hired.

Remember I said earlier that employers hire people they like. Just think about the other candidates for that position with the education and experience who did not get that job. She used a creative technique to get employers' attention and stay on their minds.

Remember these are the same people who refused to give her an interview when she first made contact with them.
Employers hire people they like! Be creative! Be liked! Get hired!
Again, this does not mean that these creative techniques will work 100 percent of the time. These experiences I am sharing with you are to motivate your creative mind so you can come up with some creative ideas to stand

out in the minds of employers. Don't give up. You may want to get creative ideas from other people. Try friends, relatives, neighbors, or even children.

Children have very creative minds. One former student of mine used to go home each day after class and share with his preteen son what he learned in class, how he was applying it, and the results. Well, after an interview, his son reminded him he had to say thank you with a thank-you letter. The boy also told him he should be creative since he learned this in class. Dad asked his son if he had any ideas to be creative. The son said yes. Since Dad was into construction and they didn't have a lot of money, he should accompany the thank-you letter with a key chain with a miniature replica of a wrench or hammer attached.

It worked. After dropping the letter and key chain off to one of the bosses at the construction site and walking out of the trailer office, he was called back in. He was told "No one ever says thank you around here. Even when people get hired, they don't say thank you. Instead, they strike when things don't go their way." The next words were the words he wanted to hear: "I like you; I'm gonna hire you." You see, that company was being threatened with a strike at that time. But that student got hired.
Again, employers hire people they like! Be creative! Be liked! Get hired!

CHAPTER 7
MARKETING YOURSELF EFFECTIVELY

A word fitly spoken is like apples of gold in pictures of silver.

How you market yourself is key to getting an interview. It will lead you into setting up or scheduling an interview, which is an important part of the job search. So please don't take it lightly. To market yourself means to sell yourself. That's sometimes done in stages.

For example, the direct contact process is one area where you can begin the marketing process. Direct contact can be done by telephone, email, or walking in.

We call this cold-calling. Whichever method of direct contact you use is your choice. I suggest you use a variety of methods so your job search doesn't become dull and boring. You want to keep your search fresh and enjoyable.

So, let us start with phone calling. First make sure you have a list of numbers, which can be obtained from various sources. What are some of the resources you can utilize to get telephone numbers? There are many resources, including

- telephone and business-to-business directories;
- the internet;
- news classifieds;
- chambers of commerce;

- economic development organizations;
- local development corporations; and
- bulletin boards.

These are just a few of the resources you can use to obtain numbers. Once you have your numbers, then make sure you have pens, pencils with erasers (someone may give you additional information or you may need to do some corrections), a notepad, and of course a telephone.

You may have in mind what you're going to say. When cold-calling, you'll be engaging individuals who did not invite you to contact them. I would suggest you ask them the questions listed in the next chapter regarding setting up an interview. Usually they will volunteer this kind of information because it is pertinent information to you having a successful interview. But just in case, what do you do if someone says, "Yes, I have a position open?"

After you've spoken with someone and they say they do have a position, you'll want to set up an interview. In the next chapter, I've listed the questions you need to ask. If the individual you're talking to misses something, you have the right questions prepared for you to set up an interview properly: *Who? What? Where? When? and How?*

Setting up the interview properly is important. Let me show why I say this. I've seen interviewees open up an interview improperly because, when setting up the interview, they didn't get all the vital information that would have made the introduction into the interview more effective. Remember people are in business to make money; time is money in the business world. The last thing you want to do is annoy a potential employer by talking too much while they're trying to focus their attention on too many things. You need to get and hold their attention for sixty seconds or less in order to whet their appetite about you, and then schedule the interview. Please leave all the details about yourself for an interview, where you have their undivided attention.

I suggest using "the sixty-second offer technique." Before scheduling the interview, please briefly make them an offer after a brief introduction.

Too many times I've seen and heard people ask for a job before offering the employer something of value. That is not selling yourself; that's panhandling. Selling yourself is like selling anything else: you tell the benefits of having what it is you're trying to sell. If you're selling a car, you tell the potential buyer it will get them where they want to go faster and safer. If you are selling fruits, you tell them it is healthy for them and their loved ones. If you're selling kitchen appliances, you tell them it will free up some of the time they used to spend in the kitchen and allow them more time to do the things they really want to do.

Similarly, when you're selling yourself to a potential employer, you want them to know the benefits of having you work for them. For example, employers can benefit from the benefits detailed in the following lists.

Your Education:

- experience (work related)
- licenses
- training (on the job)
- volunteer experience
- diplomas, certificates, degrees, college credits

Your Qualities:

- reliability
- following directions
- good communication
- hardworking
- self-motivation

Your Skills:

- operating equipment/machinery
- maintaining equipment/machinery
- reducing costs
- increasing revenue

All these facets can benefit an employer.

As mentioned earlier, at the initial contact, you should make an offer. The best way to offer the employer the benefits to be obtained by hiring you is to offer your education, experience, and qualities in sixty seconds or less.

I've created a script that will help you make the offer on the first contact. I emphasize saving all the good juicy details about yourself for the interview, when their undivided attention is on you and you only.

Introduction on a Cold Call

Hello, my name is_____.
What is the name of your hiring manager?
Ms./Mr. _____?
May I speak with Ms./Mr. _____?
Thank You.
Make an Offer (any one of the following three):
Mr./Ms. _____, my name is _____.

1) **Experience**
I have _____ years experience as a _____.

2) **Qualities and Skills**
I am hardworking and have been known to reduce costs for others in this industry due to my ability to maintain and operate a _____ machine.

3) **Education**
I have a certificate/degree/license in _____.

After the Offer, Name the Position You Want

Do you have a position for a _____ available? You can broaden your request for the position, for example: Do you have available a position for a receptionist or any other office-related position?

For offer #2, you can offer skills or qualities or a combination of both.

For offer #3, I suggest you offer one or two items if they are both related to the job you're going after.

Keep in mind that most employers will prefer you to go online to submit a résumé rather than walk into their place of business. As discussed earlier, use your cover letter effectively.

CHAPTER 8
EFFECTIVE INTERVIEW TECHNIQUES

When using the direct cold call approach outlined in the previous chapter, over the telephone you can read the script over the phone word for word and then fill in the blanks with the necessary personal information.

Since you can use this same script when walking in to someone's place of business to seek employment, it would be good practice for you to read it over and over again on the phone. You'll memorize it and you won't have to walk in to a business and read your presentation to them. That would really look awful.

The most effective way to use this script is to practice first. I suggest, besides taping yourself, to have someone listen to you for your first ten contacts and ask them to give you serious feedback. After you have received helpful criticism and made the changes needed, you can tape yourself and play it back to listen to how you sound.

Meditate on how it sounds to you while putting yourself in the place of the person on the other side of the phone. I know we are our own worst critics, so be kind but honest with yourself.

After you have completed at least twenty-one sixty-second presentations from the script on the telephone, you're ready to walk in to someone's place of business and repeat the exact same script without the text in front of you. Now you see why I suggest using the telephone first. It gives you time to practice what to say when you are in front of a potential employer.

After you follow the above script, someone will likely say, "Yes, we have job openings or positions available." Below is the information you need to collect.

When scheduling an interview in person or via electronic media, attempt to complete the following steps.

1. Get the *name of the interviewer*. What better way to impress the interviewer at the beginning of the interview than to use their name in the introduction?
2. Find out *what you should take to the interview*. Now we all know to take the following items:

   - five résumés
   - master application
   - two black pens and two #2 pencils
   - notepad or writing paper
   - two pieces of ID (state ID, Social Security card)

But there may be other important things they'll need before they can hire you. I've seen situations where the employer liked the interviewee so much they wanted to hire them immediately but couldn't because they needed to bring some sort of document back before they could be hired. Now imagine that's you. You go home, retrieve your documents, and return the next day with excitement and enthusiasm, but you then find out the position has been filled. Many things could occur between the time you left and returned with those documents.

Suppose the boss found out after you left that his nephew needed work. So he takes precedence over you. You're out; he's in. That's because you didn't secure that job as soon as possible. Use every opportunity in your powers to reduce any risk of not getting the job.

If you are familiar with the industry in which you're applying, you may have an idea of what's needed. So take the lead in asking whether you should bring any of the following:

- driving abstract
- results of a physical
- license
- portfolio
- certifications
- degrees/diploma

Make sure you find out *what you are to bring* with you to the interview. It could sometimes make a big difference.

3. Is there more information you need to get from them? Well, have you found out *where the interview will be held?*
4. Knowing where it will be held, *when will the interview be held?*
5. *How can you get there?* This is crucial to you getting to your interview on time while keeping the anxiety level down, making your interview a little more relaxing and at the same time increasing your confidence.

I want to share one experience I witnessed while I was contracted with a New York City HRA contract vendor.

A participant came back from an interview with an expression of anger on his face. Of course I was expecting a different look, being that he was returning from an interview he and I both had been anticipating with excitement for an entire week. I thought maybe something happened between leaving the interview and his arrival back to the job search class. I thought bringing the success of the interview back to his mind might relieve his mind of whatever was causing him to display such an uncomfortable look. I was wrong, dead wrong. Not knowing his dilemma, in a cheerful tone I asked, "How did things go at the interview?"

He answered, "They didn't interview me." His next statement told me he knew what I was going to ask when my mouth opened. Before the words came out, he was answering, "They said I came too late so somebody else got the job."

I'm quite sure my facial expression was changing and was probably close to matching his look, but I was about to find out it was for totally different reasons. Was I really feeling a burning in my chest as if I was in need of oxygen, or was I just imagining this feeling? Not being ready for his reply to my next question is what put me in this emotional state of mind. I could not believe the next few words that came from this young man's mouth, which seemed to wrap a pair of long claws around my throat and squeeze with a tight grip. After I asked him if he was late, his astonishing reply was, "Yeah!"

But that did not bother me as much as the rest of his statement. His next words are what rocked me. He nearly finished me off by saying, "Shoot. I didn't know how to get there. I thought if I left my house an hour before the interview, I could find it. Plus I was only three hours late. They didn't have to play me like that. They could've waited."

I wanted to know why he didn't know how to get there when he set up the interview himself and we made sure that he had an unlimited metro card that he could use on a city bus or the subway system. But at this time it was useless to ask any more questions. I figured that wouldn't help the situation at all. Even with the best of coaches, you won't learn everything about job searches all at once. And I for one know mistakes, if handled properly, can lead to growth.

Before I knew it, my head was spinning. I had to check my thoughts in order to say the right things. My mind raced back over the last few weeks of work that the team and I put into this man for job search preparation. At the same time, I was thinking maybe this was a good thing. He needed more attention when it came to proper attitude.

What should and could he have done to prevent being late?

See, I realized at that point what he was supposed to do. He was supposed to ask the person he set up the interview with for directions or ask them which train or bus stop was near them. Then he could have contacted the NYC transit authority and received direction from them. Once this young man got the directions, he would have had a whole week from the time he set up the interview to the actual interview to do test runs by the location of the interview. Prior to the interview date, he should and could have tried various ways to get there, seeing which route was the quickest.

Remember I spoke earlier about being organized and having a schedule. If you have to do test runs to find the fastest way to get to a location, please factor this into your schedule.

The key point here is *get the directions to the interview*. As a reminder, I will admit it: the mistake was not his, it was mine, because I am the coach and I overlooked a very important aspect of the job search. Prior to this experience, I did not emphasize the importance of getting directions and doing test runs by the interview location. And like any good coach, I had to own up. I apologized, too, and told him that everything was going to be all right. Because we were going back to the drawing board and perfecting our job search techniques and skills.

Oh, by the way, that young man soon after that did get a job, and I never made that mistake again. From that point on, getting directions to the interview was always factored into my lesson on setting up the interview. As I said, mistakes lead to growth.

Here is the list of questions you need answered:

- Who will interview me? (Name)
- What should I bring? (Documents)
- Where will the interview be held? (Location)
- When will it be held? (Day/Time)
- How do I get there? (Directions)

Proper Interview Opening

Sayings of Wisdom

If you understand the beginning well, the end will not trouble you.
—Ashanti proverb

Every aspect of your job search is about you selling yourself until you're fully employed. It's in the interview where you sell, sell, sell. Your approach to the interview must leave a positive lasting impression on the interviewer. Take control by opening the interview properly.

As your job search coach, I must tell you I am not speaking of the hundredth percentile. Everything I tell you is not written in stone, but I want to give you the basic foundation and reduce the risk factors. The reason I'm telling you this now is because we are now going to discuss opening the interview. Not every interview will be the same.

Before I give you the basic interview opening for a formal interview, let me mention an interview where if you're not experienced, you won't know where your interview began or ended.

The waiting room area interview is usually where the person at the front desk is there to watch, observe, listen, and determine whether the candidates for the positions are the right people or not. Later, I am going to tell you some other things that can happen in the waiting room concerning you getting that job.

But for right now, I've listed some dos for the interview:

- Start with the interviewer's name.
- Offer a handshake.
- Keep good eye contact.
- Introduce yourself.
- State the position you're interviewing for.
- Offer your résumé/application.
- Remain standing until invited to sit.

If you were not invited to sit down immediately after the introduction, it's okay to take the initiative to ask, "May I sit down?" Keep in mind that not every interview or interviewer will be the same, so sometimes the opening may vary.

One of the most important elements to opening the interview is the handshake. What would you do if an interviewer refused to shake your hand?

Do not look startled or appear raddled if an interviewer does not respond to you offering your hand for a professional handshake. Some people refuse to shake hands for religious or cultural reasons or phobias. If it is for any of these reasons, more than likely they will explain.

However in many cases when a potential employer refuses to shake your hand, it's just to test you.

I'll give you an example of what I'm talking about. Let's say an employer, we'll call him Mr. Brown, has three good workers: Bill, Bob, and Sue. They bring in 80 percent of his profits. They've each been with him for fifteen years.

The problem is they are rude and obnoxious to other good employees and chase them away. And let's say he would have to hire ten people to bring in the kind of money these three bring in.

It's hard for Mr. Brown to keep other workers, but he's not getting rid of these money getters. So any time someone comes to Mr. Brown to apply for a job, he tests them out to see if they'll be able to work with his three obnoxious moneymakers. One test he might use is the handshake test. You come into the interview all excited and positive, ready to go through the opening, the interview introduction that I've prepared for you. You reach your hand out to shake his hand while applying the eye contact technique in expectation of him giving you a firm handshake. Instead, he steps back and looks down at your hand as though it was just used as a pooper-scooper.

What would you do? Well, no need to panic now that you know about the handshake test. While smiling just drop your hand back down to your side without missing a beat to your rhythm as you continue your verbal part of the "open the interview" introduction.

Never, for any reason, show any signs of anger or frustration in or around an interview. If you can't handle not having your hand shook, more than likely you wouldn't be able to handle what his three money getters have in store for you. So it makes no sense to hire you.

There are many ways to test you. Since we're talking about tests, here are a few more tests you might encounter.

Remember I said wait to be seated. I also said you could ask if you may sit down. Some interviewers have been known not to invite you to be seated. This test is sometimes used to see if you are presumptuous.

I passed this test myself while interviewing for a job as a job search coach. One particular interviewer, after the introduction, left me standing, sat down, looked down at the paper on his desk, and began asking me questions. He didn't look up while I answered. After I answered the first question, I asked him if he minded me sitting as I gestured to the chair. He immediately apologized for not offering me the seat. Approximately fifteen minutes into the interview, after asking him one of my questions, he informed me the position was available because the person who held it formerly was presumptuous in making decisions that he had no authority to make. Because I knew the individual who once held this position and many of the workers still working there at that time, I was quite aware of why the position was available. So with this information coupled with knowledge of the industry, I figured I would be tested on the very things we teach. Of course I passed that test and, along with my background and interviewing skills, got the job.

Another test employers have used on occasions is to leave candidates sitting alone over a period of time to see if the individual is patient and can follow directions.

Earlier I said I was going to tell you about some things going on in some waiting rooms. The waiting room test is when they leave various types of literature spread out for your choosing. One will always be about the particular job or industry you are going for or information on their company, the company you're applying to work for. Then there will be other literature. Maybe there will be magazines on sports, hobbies, nightlife, religion, or politics.

Believe me, someone, usually the receptionist, is watching to see exactly what your interests are at this time. If you're going to read something to pass the time, I suggest picking up the literature on the company or a magazine about the industry you're contemplating going into or something closely related.

If you didn't know it, now you know that in many cases, your waiting time in the waiting area is part of your interview process. Give them what they want, not what you think they want.

Employers and hiring managers have the right and many reasons to test you. Accept that fact. To be forewarned is to be forearmed. Employers in whatever business they're in want to hire a person who is solely interested in *the job, the company, and the industry* to which they themselves are committed. So if you're not getting any hiring offers, it is because you're not selling yourself properly somewhere in your job search. You need to show them that you have a hard-core interest in one or more of the three things I just told you would make them like you and hire you. You'll have another opportunity to show what your interests are. That opportunity comes in the interview and may be the last chance you'll have.

The Interview (Formal Sit-Down)

The key to a successful interview is

- have a theme;
- prepare;

- practice; and
- listen carefully to the questions asked.

By this point in your job search, you should *have a theme* to your interview.

Each job interview is different, the employers are different, the companies are different, and the types of jobs you are interviewing for may be different as well as the industries. That means your themes for your interviews will not always be the same. You must prepare your theme based on your strengths, your qualities, and what you know about the position, the company, the industry, and possibly the interviewer. It sounds like a lot of work, doesn't it? Well, job searching is a job itself.

Let's begin by looking at two of the biggest mistakes that could be prevented by having and sticking to a theme. The first is: *not listening*.

The *number one error made on interviews is not listening to the questions asked*. I have seen this most times when individuals attempt to answer the most popular question most people will be asked on an interview. It is usually the first question asked. When taking a survey among my clients, this interview question has seemed to be the most difficult to answer. By now you've probably guessed what question I'm talking about. It is "Would you please tell me something about yourself?"

I've found that the majority of job seekers who mess that one up is because they don't listen to the question. Keep in mind in most cases when you are called in for an interview, it's after an employer has already looked at your résumé.

During the interview, usually the interviewer will have your résumé in their hand. (When you opened the interview, you should have offered your résumé unless the interviewer has already indicated they have your résumé with them.)

So you want to ask yourself, "What is the interviewer looking for when he says, 'Tell me something about yourself please'?" Some who don't listen to the question and reason on the matter will begin the second mistake, which is *reading the résumé*.

Reading off job descriptions already read by the interviewer from the résumé is not good.

The interviewer already went over your résumé and thought you could perform or learn to perform the duties the position requires. Why should anyone sit there and read your former job description again, this time with you?

Matter of fact, why would someone sit there and listen to you tell them what they already know? Time is money in the business world. We are already dealing with a slow economy. Why deal with a slow interviewee?

If you waste the employer's time, some may consider not hiring you from that point on. This is how employers think: if you can't listen to the question carefully now, you may not listen to it after you're hired. The ability to follow directions is the leading quality an employer looks for in a potential employee. Following directions requires listening carefully.

I can prevent a lot of problems later by not hiring this person who hasn't listened to or answered my question. I could put myself at risk of losing a lot if I hired such a person. How can this person satisfy my customers' needs (external and internal customers) if he or she can't listen?

Am I saying it is wrong to talk about past jobs and the duties you performed on those jobs? Am I saying that to use past jobs when answering this question would mean you are not listening to the question? Far from it.

The third top mistake I beg you please to not do is to go into an interview and tell an interviewer, "I'll be an asset to your company" and leave it up to them to guess how. *That would not be the right sales approach.*

People who are in business want to do three things: make money, save money, and enhance the image of their company. Once you can describe to them how you will accomplish one or more of these, with past experiences from previous employment to back up your claim, you won't have to say you'll be an asset. They will see for themselves that you will be an asset.

Here is an example script of a job seeker interviewing for a nurse's aide position (after certification training and no previous employment experience as a nurse's aide).

Interviewer: Mr. White, why should we hire you?

Mr. White: As you see on my résumé, my past work experience is as a dietary aide. It was there I learned to read patients' charts. I learned what the color codes meant on the dietary charts and food trays. So if you hire me today, none of your patients could manipulate me into giving them foods they are not supposed to have. This would *reduce the risk of lawsuits and in turn would save you money.*

Before addressing what the interviewer wants and how you should deliver it to them, let me tell you the fourth common mistake made trying to answer "Tell me something about yourself." This is where people go up and down the "*I am* ladder"—talking about nothing, saying a lot of "I am this, I am that, people say I am this, some say that I am that …"

Do you have any idea what kind of problem this could cause you on an interview? After you spent time and energy finding a potential employer, setting up the interview, getting ready, and traveling to the interview, now you've caused him to stop listening to you. Yes, they will stop listening to you when they have to start asking themselves questions in their head about something you said. Here are some examples:
If he is hardworking, where was he hardworking?
What did he do that was so hard?
How long was she hardworking?
Who benefited from her hard work?
How did anyone benefit from her hard work?
Or if she is a team player, what team was she on?
What position did she hold on the team?
What was the goal of the team?
How effective was she in carrying out her part for the team?

That's a lot of questions for one to be asking themselves just because someone went into an interview, got up on the "*I am* ladder," and said, "I am hardworking. I am a team player. I am, I am, I am," with absolutely no colorful elaboration.

When you are asked to tell something about yourself, the interviewer wants to know who you are as a person. They want to know whether you will fit in with the company's goals, staff, and their customers, clients, residents, or patients. Their main concern is in what way you will benefit the company.

So when bringing up past jobs to answer this question, please talk about these past jobs as to how they have made you the person you are today and how they made you the right person for the position. Tell them how your past job duties prepared you for the job you're now applying for. Let them know what qualities and skills you took to those past jobs and what qualities and skills you developed at those past jobs and how they benefited the previous employers. Be sure to inform them on how your qualities and skills grew on your past jobs. Let them know which ones you are bringing to their company if hired and how these qualities and skills will enhance your job performance and how they would benefit their company.

Be descriptive. Paint a full colorful picture of yourself on past jobs so they'll be able to see you at work in uniform handling those clients, patients, or customers.

You can do this easily by incorporating your *theme* and using your theme from the beginning right down to the end of your interview. Sticking to your theme will give you a foundation and help you stay in control of the interview. No matter what question is asked of you, you'll bring them right back to the idea you want to convey about yourself through your theme.

You may be asking yourself in bewilderment, "Am I going to be saying the same thing throughout the entire interview?"

Keep in mind you are on *your* interview. Your interview is your show. Your audience is the interviewer or interviewers. Every show has a *theme*. TV, movies, Broadway plays, stand-up comedy, and motivational and public speaking all have a *theme* that runs from beginning to end, and so should your show, your interview. You don't have to say the same words over and over again, but the same idea can be expressed various ways.

Let me start by showing you an example of answering the question "Would you please tell me about yourself?" using a *theme*. I will use the nurse's aide interview for our example.

First I selected a *theme* based on my knowledge of the job and industry and what qualities and skills I have that are needed to do the job. Follow me carefully because you must do the same.

My knowledge and experience of the position and industry dictate to me that for this particular interview, I should use *Team Player* as my theme. (Keep in mind there are other themes you can use.)

I practiced prior to the interview to get the idea in my head. I don't want to get stuck on words. I will not say the words *team* or *team player* throughout the entire interview. However, I can and will use words, phrases, experiences, and illustrations that mean "team player."

That is what I want for you. That's why practice is imperative. Get the idea that the theme conveys in your head. This way you'll sound like your natural self. Also, you will be able to stay in control of the interview if you stick to your theme.

Now in this way, I can relax a little and be myself in the interview. My chosen theme is "Team Player." So here it goes

Interviewer: Would you please tell me something about yourself?

Me: I'm a team player. The reason I can confidently say this is because I have worked for three years as a nurse's aide at Brookdale University Hospital. There I worked in unity with the doctors, nutritionists, therapists, and nurses to get the patients the proper care that they needed and deserved.

Due to budget cuts, there were times when a coworker could not be on the floor with their patients. They did not have to worry about their patients as long as I was there. They knew and respected the fact that I would take care of their patients right along with mine until they could return.

This attitude, among other things, enhanced the image of the hospital among patients and their families, and we soon became the crème de la crème among hospital care. This contributed to an increase in profits, which is what I intend to do for this facility if you were to hire me today.

The interviewer did not have to ask herself what team I was on. I told her (medical).

She did not have to ask where or how long. I was clear on where and how long (three years at Brookdale University Hospital).

She did not need to ask herself what the goal of the team was. Since every team is constructed to accomplish a goal, I as a team member should know the goal. If I'm telling the truth about being a team player, I should know the team's goals or mission. I did inform her our goal was to get the patients the proper care that they needed and deserved.

Since every member on a team has particular duties to carry out for the team to be effective, I even informed her on how effective I was in carrying out my part for the team—so effective my team members could count on me to step in and take care of their patients for them when they were not available.

Now I want to make a brief point just to show you how important a theme could be. This demonstrates what I mean by a theme helps you stay in control of your interview. You know I did not go up and down on that "*I am* ladder" checking off "I am this, and I am that." I made the interviewer go up and down, checking off qualities she heard other than team player.

Most likely she heard that I was

- responsible;

- reliable;
- empathetic;
- a good communicator;
- a people person; and
- hardworking.

When you use your theme and talk about it, the interviewer will hear all those other good qualities about you without you putting your interview at risk of losing them.

Below I have included two lists of interview questions and prompts commonly used at interviews. Keep in mind every item is about the position you're seeking and should be answered accordingly.

Common Interview Questions

1. Please tell me something about yourself.
2. What can you bring to this company?
3. What is your biggest achievement?
4. What is your biggest weakness?
5. What do you expect as a starting salary?
6. Why should we hire you?
7. Why do you want to work for us?
8. Where do you expect to be in five years?
9. Do you have any questions for me?

Trendy Behavioral Interview Questions

In a job interview, most likely you will encounter behavioral interview questions. Find out more about this type of interview question, review the most common behavioral interview questions employers ask, and learn how to prepare and respond smoothly when you're asked to give examples of how you handle workplace situations.

Why Are Behavioral Interview Questions Important to Employers?

In contrast to traditional interview questions that ask you to describe what you did in a position or to share your qualifications, these questions are used to probe for concrete examples of skills and experiences that relate directly to the position.

Questions are generally formed by presenting a situation. The interviewer may inquire about what action you took to respond to something similar in the past and what the result was.

The interviewer will ask how you handled a particular type of situation, and you will need to explain what you did. The logical idea is that your success in the past is a positive indicator of your success in the future.

Ten Common Behavioral Interview Questions Sample Answers That Work

Below we list common behavioral interview questions you may be asked during a job interview. Review the responses and consider how you would answer the questions based on your own experiences.

As you can see from the sample responses, it's important to be ready with specific examples. While you don't need to memorize answers, have a sense of what experiences you would share and how to describe them to the interviewer. You'll want your examples to be both clear and easy to follow.

1. Tell me about how you worked effectively under pressure.
   What employers want to know

   If you're being considered for a high-stress job, the interviewer will want to know how well you can work under pressure. Give a real example of how you've dealt with pressure when you respond.

Response

We were in the middle of complicated negotiations with a new sponsor. I had been working on a key project that was scheduled for delivery to the client in sixty days. My supervisor came to me and said that we needed to speed it up and be ready in forty-five days while keeping our other projects on time. I made it into a challenge for my staff, and we effectively added just a few hours to each of our schedules and got the job done in forty-two days by sharing the workload. Of course, I had a talented group of people to work with, but I think that my effective allocation of tasks was a major contribution to the success of the project.

Cross-exam question: How do you handle stress?

Cross-exam questions usually call for elaboration on a previous question.

2. How do you handle a challenge? Give an example.
   What employers want to know

   Regardless of your job, things may go wrong, and it won't always be business as usual. With this type of question, the hiring manager wants to know how you will react in a difficult situation. When you respond, focus on how you resolved a challenging situation.

   Response

   One time my supervisor needed to leave town unexpectedly, and we were putting together a PowerPoint presentation just from the notes he had left and some briefing from his manager. My presentation turned out successfully. We got the sponsorship, and the management team even recommended me for an award.

   Cross-exam question: Tell me about how you handled a challenging situation.

3. Since no one is perfect, how do you handle mistakes? *What employers want to know*
   Nobody is perfect, and we all make mistakes. The interviewer is more interested in how you handled it when you made an error, rather than in the fact that it happened.

   Response

   I once misquoted the fees for a particular type of membership to the club where I worked. I explained my mistake to my supervisor, who appreciated my coming to him and my honesty. He told me to offer to waive the application fee for the new member. The member joined the club despite my mistake, my supervisor was understanding, and although I felt bad that I had made a mistake, I learned to pay close attention to the details so as to be sure to give accurate information in the future.

   Tip: How to answer interview questions about mistakes.

4. On a one-to-ten scale, how important is goal setting to you? *What employers want to know*

   With this question, the interviewer wants to know how well you plan and set goals for what you want to accomplish. The easiest way to respond is to share examples of successful goal setting.

   Response

   Within a few weeks of beginning my first job as a sales associate in a department store, I knew that I wanted to be in the fashion industry. I decided that I would work my way up to department manager, and at that point, I would have enough money saved to be able to attend design school full-time. I did just that, and I even landed my first job through an internship I completed the summer before graduation. So on a one-to-ten scale, goal setting is very high for me. Maybe an eleven.

5. Give an example of a goal you reached, and tell me how you achieved it.
What employers want to know

What they are asking is what you would do to achieve your goals and the steps you would take to accomplish them.

Response

As indicated on my résumé, I worked for ABC Company, which offered a motivational challenge. Very few employees took it seriously. But I did because I really wanted that parking spot and my picture on the wall. I went out of my way to be helpful to my coworkers, supervisors, and customers, which was the norm for me in any work capacity. The third month I was there, I got the honor. It was good to achieve my goal, and I actually ended up moving into a managerial position within six months of my start date. I think it was because of my positive attitude, perseverance, and customer service skills.

6. Describe a decision you made that wasn't popular, and explain how you handled implementing it.
What employers want to know

Sometimes management has to make difficult decisions, and not all employees are happy when a new policy is put in place. If you're interviewing for a decision-making role, the interviewer will want to know your process for implementing change.

Response

Once I accepted a leadership position working with a group of employees when their supervisor relocated to another city. They had been allowed to cover one another's shifts without management approval. There were inconsistencies, where certain people were being given more opportunities than others. I thought this was an unfair practice that could lead to a breakdown in team morale, so

I introduced a policy where I had my assistant approve all staffing changes, to make sure that everyone who wanted extra hours and was available at certain times could be utilized. The team saw me as a fair leader.

Cross-exam question: What are the most difficult decisions to make?

7. Give an example of how you worked on a team.
   What employers want to know

   Many jobs require working as part of a team. In interviews for those roles, the hiring manager will want to know how well you work with others and cooperate with other team members.

   Response

   While in college, I worked as part of a research team in the XYZ department. The professor leading the project was writing a book on the development of language in Europe in the Middle Ages. We were each assigned different sectors to focus on, and I suggested that we meet independently before our weekly meeting with the professor to discuss our progress and help one another out if we were having any difficulties. The professor really appreciated the way we worked together, and it helped to streamline his research as well. He started on his final copy months ahead of schedule because of our team effort.

8. What do you do if you disagree with someone at work?
   What employers want to know

   With this question, the interviewer is seeking insight into how you handle issues at work. Focus on how you've solved a problem or compromised when there was a workplace disagreement.

Response

A few years ago, I had a supervisor who wanted me to find ways to outsource most of the work we were doing in my department. I felt having the staff on premises had a huge impact on our effectiveness and ability to relate to our clients. I presented a strong case to her, and she came up with a compromise plan I gladly accepted.

9. Share an example of how you were able to motivate employees or coworkers.
   What employers want to know

   Do you have strong motivational skills? What strategies do you use to motivate your team? The hiring manager is looking for a concrete example of your ability to motivate others.

   Response

   I was in a situation once where the management of our department was taken over by employees with experience in a totally different industry in an effort to maximize profits over service. Many of my coworkers were resistant to the sweeping changes that were being made, but I immediately recognized some of the benefits and was able to motivate my colleagues by explaining the pros and cons and how the entire company would benefit if we cooperated in giving the new process a chance to succeed. It worked. We reached our profit goal by the fourth quarter and saw a 4 percent increase. Everyone appreciated receiving a bonus.

10. Have you handled a difficult situation? How?
    What employers want to know

    Can you handle difficult situations at work, or do you not deal with them well? The employer will want to know what you do when there's a problem.

Response

When I worked at ABC International Corporation, it came to my attention that one of our employees had become addicted to painkillers prescribed after she had surgery. Her performance was being negatively impacted, and she needed help. I thanked the employee who brought it to my attention. To avoid gossip and slander, I put together a short department workshop on the theme of integrity. Prior to putting together the workshop, I spoke privately with our employee who was suffering, and I helped her to arrange a weekend treatment program that was covered by her insurance. Fortunately, she was able to get her life back on track, and she received a promotion about six months later.

Possible Follow-Up Questions

- Have you worked on multiple projects? How did you prioritize?
- How do you handle meeting tight deadlines?
- How do you handle it when your schedule is interrupted?
- What do you do if you disagree with a coworker?
- Give me an example of when you did or when you didn't listen.
- What do you do if you disagree with your boss?
- How do you handle it when there's a conflict among team members?
- What is your most important career accomplishment? Why?

How to Prepare for a Behavioral Interview

- Learn about the company and the role. The more you know about the job and the company, the easier it will be to respond to interview questions.

- Take the time to research the company prior to your interview and review the job posting so you're as familiar as possible with the role.
- Match your qualifications to the job.

  1. Review the job requirements.
  2. Make a list of the behavioral skills that you have that closely match them.
  3. Make a list of examples. Interviewers develop questions to determine how successful a candidate will be given the specific tasks of the job. Obviously, you want to present your experiences as clearly as you can, using real examples and highlighting situations where you were successful. Be ready to share a story. You may be asked variations of the questions listed above, but if you prepare some stories to share with the interviewer, you'll be able to readily respond.

Make the Best Impression

Before you head out to your interview, review these tips and strategies for behavioral interview success. Be sure you have questions of your own ready to ask the interviewer and are prepared to follow up after the interview with a thank-you note (as discussed in other chapters). Use your theme from the beginning all the way through to the end of your interview. This will take you into the proper closing technique.

Proper Closing of the Interview

This is the part of the interview where the interviewer says to you, "Thank you, Ms./Mr. _____. We'll get back to you within two weeks and let you know what our decision is."

How do you close this interview? What do you say and do at this point? Here is another opportunity to set yourself aside from most job seekers.

This is done by closing with your theme. Use a word or words that connect with your theme. Look at the following list of closing examples.

Theme: Team Player
Close: (Shake hands.) Thank you, Ms./Mr. _____. Hire me; I really would like to be a part of your team.

Theme: Reliable
Close: (Shake hands.) Thank you, Ms./Mr. _____. Hire me; you and your clients can *rely* on me.

Theme: Hardworking
Close: (Shake hands.) Thank you, Ms./Mr. _____. Hire me, and I will *work hard* for your company.

Theme: Trustworthy
Close: (Shake hands.) Thank you, Ms./Mr. _____. Hire me; you and your customers can *trust* me.

Theme: Customer Service
Close: (Shake hands.) Thank you, Ms./Mr. _____. Hire me, and I'll *wow* your customers with excellent customer service skills.

Theme: Make Money
Close: (Shake hands.) Thank you, Ms./Mr. _____. Hire me, and I'll …

increase your revenue.
or
increase your profits.
or
make you money.

These are just a few examples of how to properly close an interview. The reason you want to use this method is because the last thing said before you walk out of that interview will be the first thing remembered about you.

You want the employer to connect right away to the things you told them about you in the interview. So after you close, I suggest you don't say anything else at all. Just walk out. Leave them with the last words lingering.

CHAPTER 9

HOW TO FOLLOW UP ON THE INTERVIEW

Following up on the interviews is as important as any other part of your job search. My years of job search coaching have taught me that most job seekers don't follow up on the interview, and of those who do, only a few know how to do so effectively.

In this chapter I will show you how it should be done and why you should do the things I describe to you in this chapter.

The first step is to refer back to chapter 5 under the subheading "Thank-You Letter." This is the tool you will need in following up on your interview. That chapter helps you put together a thank-you letter. Many job seekers will email their thank-you letter. I suggest you take your thank-you letter by hand to the interviewer.

If you cannot get in to see the interviewer directly, make sure you leave the letter with a responsible person such as a receptionist, administrative assistant, or personal assistant. Make it clear verbally and in writing who the letter is to go to. Also be sure you have the name and position of the person you're giving this responsibility to.

Now let's get to the reason I suggest taking the letter in person. When you went to the interview, you should have attempted to start building professional working relationships with anyone you could who works for that company.

For example, while waiting for the interview you could have started a brief conversation with the front desk receptionist. The conversation should have stayed professional. You could use questions about their service to the company. Here's an example of how it could have been done.

Excuse me. (Compliment them on the work they're doing.)

I know you're working, but can I take a moment to ask how long you have worked here?
Answer....................................

What do you like most and what do you like least about your job?
Answer......................................

My final question is if you could change one thing about this company, what would that be?
Answer.......................................

Thank them for their time. Tell them you look forward to working with this company and finishing the discussion. Thank them for their time again.

While waiting to be interviewed, you may be able to engage more than one employee of this company by using these same brief questions and compliments. The more people you engage, the more professional relationships you are starting in this company. "Why is this important, and what does this have to do with following up on the interview?" you may be asking.

You may not get hired this go-around, but you want to increase your chances of getting the job by building relationships in the company.

When you take the thank-you letter, you get a chance to see some of the same people you started building relationships with. You get another chance to build on the relationship you already started.

Use their names, showing them you remember the names (which means they're important). Remind them of your previous conversation. If you can find a sincere reason to compliment them or their position, do it. Thank them for conversing with you and making you feel comfortable on the day of your interview. Remind them of the position you are applying for and the interviewer you're there to thank.

If you don't get hired this time, these may be the allies you need to help you get in later. If you don't get the job, stop there once or twice a month, engage these people, and become a part of the company before being hired.

One or more of these people may be the one to see your qualities and see that you have something to bring to the company. They may express it to the former interviewer. More good opinions of you could be a plus. This is what you may need to get the phone call you want—"You got the job. When can you start?"

So it is important to take your thank-you letter in person and use that opportunity to build relationships in that company. After that, follow up with a phone call to the interviewer. Let them know you left a letter for them if you did not get a chance to give it to them directly.

However, whether the interviewer received the letter from you directly or not, just briefly let them know you really appreciate them for the time they've spent with you as well as appreciating their staff members you engaged while waiting to be interviewed. Remind them why you think you make a good professional match.

CHAPTER 10
SOCIAL MEDIA AND THE JOB SEARCH

Social media is at the intersection of technology and human interaction. We are gradually shifting to websites that offer the opportunity for greater human interaction. We leave comments and share information. In general, the major social media sites associated with job searching are described below.

LinkedIn

The professional's social network, LinkedIn is the network preferred by most employers. LinkedIn is a large professional network where members connect with each other, participate in groups, and connect and interact with each other.

LinkedIn has more than five hundred million members (as of 2018) in two hundred countries and is widely viewed as the most businesslike and professional of the social networks. See *Guide to LinkedIn for Job Search* for help leveraging LinkedIn, and join the Job-Hunt Help LinkedIn Group for help with your job search in LinkedIn.

A- + LinkedIn Profile (aka Complete LinkedIn Profile) is unavoidable for successful visibility and credibility on LinkedIn. A Complete LinkedIn Profile gives you the capability to include the keywords that are essential for your job search.

An All-Star LinkedIn Profile has these elements:

A Profile Photo

- This photo should be only you (no kids, friends, or pets), looking friendly and dressed appropriately for your profession. Do *not* avoid including this photo! Without a photo on your profile, it is invisible.

Your Professional Headline

- The headline for your profile should be accurate, descriptive, and more than simply your job title and employer name (the default). The headline is an *essential* element of a successful LinkedIn Profile.

Your Location

- For LinkedIn, your location is a city and state or region, *not* your address!

An Up-to-Date Current Position

- LinkedIn gives you two thousand spaces, so you can and should describe the position in as much detail as possible. Focus on your accomplishments, which are much more than a bulleted list of "responsible for" items. Also describe your employer unless it is an extremely well-known organization.

Two Past Positions

- Again, describe each position in detail. Like the current position, you have two thousand spaces to use for each of your other jobs, too. Highlight your successes as well as those of your employer.

Your Education

- Include college degrees (or years in college), certifications, and other relevant professional training. Read *Hidden LinkedIn Networking Tool: Education* to learn more about leveraging your schools for your job search.

Your Skills (minimum of three)

- Choose the ones most relevant to you and your profession.

At Least Fifty Connections

- And more are better, of course, because you become more visible in LinkedIn search results based on the size of your LinkedIn network. If you are not in someone's network (first, second, or third degree connection), you won't be visible to them unless they have a premium/paid account.

To understand more about including the right keywords in your LinkedIn profile, read *LinkedIn SEO: How to Be Found by Recruiters on LinkedIn* and the *free* e-book *Smart Personal Branding with LinkedIn*.

Once your profile is complete, focus on keeping it up-to-date. Tweak *your keywords* to be current, reflecting your accomplishments, and focus on the job you want next.

Facebook

The largest social network, Facebook, is a social networking website that is operated and privately owned by Facebook, Inc. Users can add friends and send them messages, as well as update their personal profiles with status reports to notify friends about themselves and their activities. Additionally, users can join networks organized by city, workplace, and school or college.

With over 2 billion members worldwide (as of 2018), Facebook is the largest social network, but it has a long history of issues with member privacy (or lack thereof).

Facebook Do-Not-Dos for Job Seekers

The hazards of using Facebook while in a job search are well known. While more than 90 percent of employers and recruiters conduct a quick background check of job applicants using search engines, over 70 percent of them have rejected job seekers based on inappropriate photos, comments, and sharing on Facebook that the searches found for them.

People often reveal far too much on sites like Facebook and Twitter. If you are one of those people, clean up your act and behave in the future, or you will pay the consequences by an extended job search.

Facebook Dos for Job Seekers

Because so many employers search and/or use Facebook for their recruiting, smart job seekers can successfully leverage the visibility that Facebook gives them. They can use Facebook to demonstrate how social-media-savvy they are (an important skill in today's business world), and they can use it intelligently to also demonstrate their skills and expertise for the job they want.

Since so many employers have social media presence on Facebook and since so many of their employees use Facebook, it can become an excellent way to expand your network and connect with a new job.

Twitter

Twitter is a free social networking and microblogging service that enables its users to send and read messages known as *tweets*. Tweets are text-based posts of up to 140 characters displayed on the author's profile page and delivered to the author's subscribers, who are known as *followers*. Twitter has over 330 million "active users" (as of mid-2018). See *Guide to Twitter for Job Search* for help leveraging Twitter.

Blogs

According to Wikipedia, blogs "are usually maintained by an individual with regular entries of commentary, descriptions of events, or other material such as graphics or video. Entries are commonly displayed in reverse-chronological order."

Many blogs provide commentary or news on a particular subject; others function as more personal online diaries. A typical blog combines text, images, and links to other blogs, web pages, and other media related to its topic. The ability of readers to leave comments in an interactive format is an important part of many blogs.

The Role of Social Media in the Job Search

Social media and social networking apply in both business and private life. Naturally, as with anything social, the job search is clearly happening in social media.

- Social media has become a fast and less expensive way to do a background check before inviting a job applicant in for an interview.
- Employers search social media to verify the facts on résumés, to check out knowledge and attitudes expressed publicly, and evaluate communications skills.
- Social media is also used to *find qualified applicants*, often a faster and cheaper method of identifying good job candidates than posting a job.

LinkedIn is the number one social network for job searching. If you have time for only one social network for your job search, LinkedIn should be the one you use.

Why Is Social Media Important to Your Job Search?

According to a 2018 CareerBuilder survey,

70% of employers use social networking sites to research job candidates (on par with last year), while 7% plan to start. And that review matters: Of those that do social research, 57% have found content that caused them not to hire candidates.

Also, being "invisible" (having no social media footprint) is *not* a good solution. The CareerBuilder survey found that nearly half of employers (47.5%) say that if they can't find a job candidate online, they are *less likely to call that person* in for an interview.

Clearly social networks have been and will continue to be for a long time very important to your job search success, as the graph below illustrates, because recruiters use them consistently.

Growth of Social Recruiting

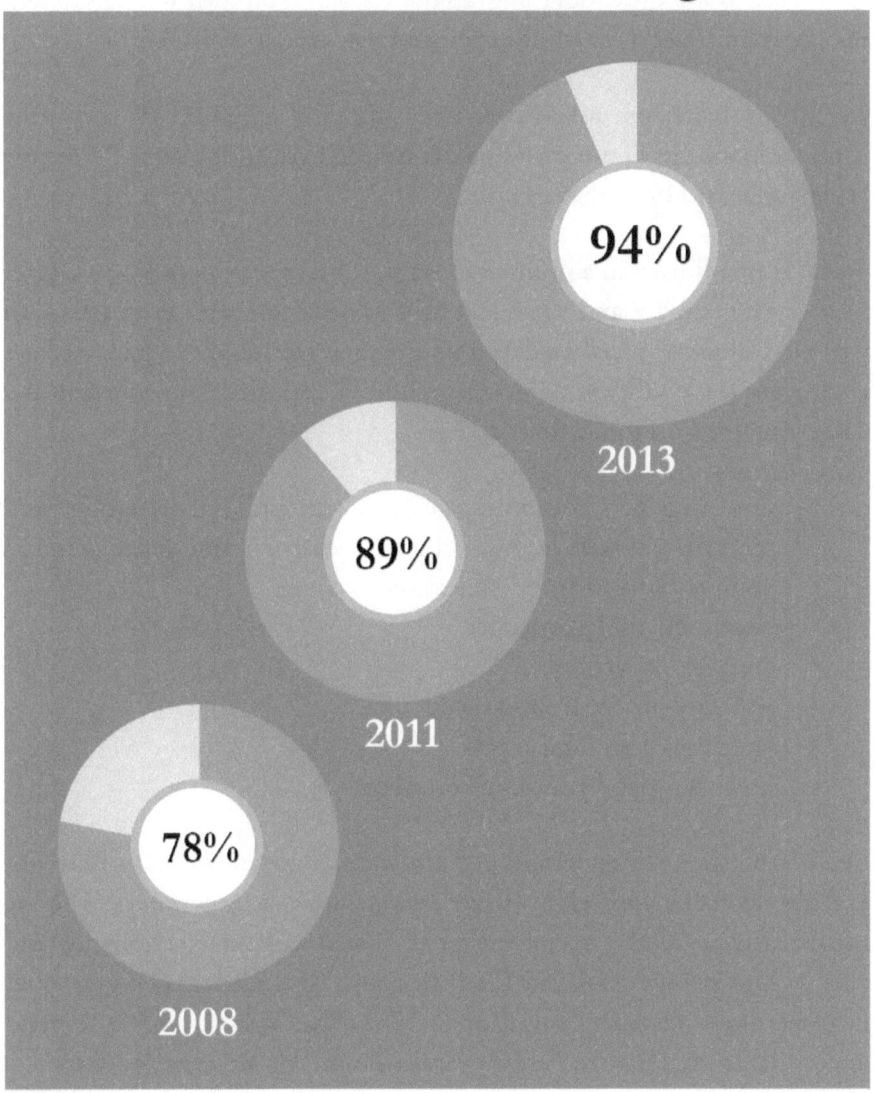

Employers and recruiters, while using job boards *less*, are using social media *more*, a trend that began before 2008 (LinkedIn had its fifteenth birthday in 2018!).

Since its inception LinkedIn has continued to dominate social networks used for recruiting. Facebook, though it is popular and liked by many, is less popular for finding job seekers, although it is used often to promote an employer as a great place to work. Besides using "About Us" pages on their websites to seek out the culture and interests of a company, you can use Facebook.

In 2013, Jobvite.com asked over eight hundred employers if they were using or planning to use social media for their recruiting, and *94 percent of employers said that yes, they would.*

Social media is used in a number of ways. It helps recruiters have a clearer idea of who you are and what you have done before they even talk with you. In your use of social media, employers and recruiters can pick up clues about your personality and how you might fit into their corporate culture. They can also gain indications of

- how well you communicate (your spelling, punctuation, and grammar, as well as your ability to clearly communicate ideas);
- your work history and education;
- your industry knowledge;
- your use of alcohol;
- your use of illegal substances;
- your use of profanity; and
- how you spend your nonwork time.

The bottom line is you should pay attention to social media to find jobs and also to make yourself available and attractive for recruiters, who are consistently searching social media to screen potential candidates and also to find people qualified for their jobs. To understand more about how recruiters are using social media and what you can do to respond appropriately, see *How to Leverage Social Recruiting for Your Job Search.*

For more information about social media's role in the job search, check out the following three books:

- Job-Hunt's *Guide to Social Media and Job Search* for information about successfully navigating all social media
- Job-Hunt's *Guide to LinkedIn for Job Search*
- Job-Hunt's *Guide to Facebook for Job Search*

ABOUT THE AUTHOR

Deirk L. Keitt Sr. was born December 16, 1959, to a single mother of four. Because of their economic situation, he often heard his mother say they barely had enough money to take care of their basic needs. So he learned early not to ask for money but instead ask for work. He would ask businesspeople in his community to employ him. Most of the time he was too young for the job, but he would convince them of the benefits in hiring and training him (if he needed training), even if it was temporary. Usually he'd get hired. Little did he know he was developing a skill that is needed by 90 percent of the world's population. That skill is how to job search, make employers like you, and get employed.

Later in life, Deirk found himself a participant in a government-sponsored job search program. He absorbed everything he learned about job searching. In three months he was hired and trained to teach job search workshops by the same company. Deirk studied job searching and interviewed job developers/recruiters, HR personnel, and job seekers. Eventually he became a job coach/counselor. He has spent a total of eighteen years in this industry growing, teaching, coaching, and helping people reach their employment goals.

ABOUT THIS MANUAL

This is an easy-to-follow manual. It is written for job seekers and those whose jobs are to help job seekers get employed. It is written in an easy-to-understand format and covers the most important factors in finding employment:

1. What you should do in the job search
2. Why you should do it
3. How you should do it

Many people find job searching very stressful. The author discusses this and makes the job search, if not so much enjoyable, at least a tolerable learning experience. When you're reading this book, you'll feel as though the author is right there with you, holding your hand through your job search.

This manual not only makes looking for employment easy for the job seeker, but it will also help those who work in the back-to-work job search industry teach, coach, and assist their job seekers reach their employment goals. There are real-life experiences from real job seekers from every walk of life shared. This book looks at people who are educated, people with limited education, people who have worked for years, and even people who have very little to no work history.

This manual also addresses

- how to organize your job search to save time;

- how to stand out as different from the rest of the job seekers; and
- techniques you can use to recruit masses of people to job search for you (you don't have to know them, and they may never know you).

These are just a few jewels among many you'll get from *America's Official Job Search Manual*. Read the book, enjoy it, get hired, and move forward with your life. I'll see you on the next level.

www.ingramcontent.com/pod-product-compliance
Lightning Source LLC
Chambersburg PA
CBHW020451220526
45464CB00002B/945